Picture book of

POLAND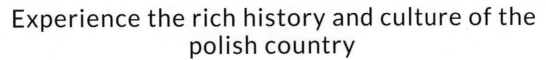

Experience the rich history and culture of the polish country

Warsaw

Poznan

Neptune Fountain in Poznan

Zakopane

Krakow

Bydgoszcz

Koscielec peak in Tatra Mountains

Gdansk

Torun

Gasienicowa valley, Tatry mountains

Poznan

Wawel castle in Krakow

Baltic sea cost

Lodz

Wild Lake in Masuria

Gdansk

Zborow mountain

Skyscrapers Warsaw

Wrocław

Kazimierz Dolny

Gdynia

Tatra mountain

Lublin

Szcecin

Pszczyna

Swinoujscie

Malbork

Kołobrzeg

Białowieża Forest

Nowy Wiśnicz

Old castle ruins of Ogrodzieniec

Krakow

Lake Ciecz

Malbork

Warsaw

Sopot

Torun

Suwalszczyna

Printed in Great Britain
by Amazon